T0067207

ROLE PLAYING

GARY BRYANT

BALBOA.
PRESS

A DIVISION OF HAY HOUSE

Balboa Press books may be ordered through booksellers or by contacting:

Balboa Press
A Division of Hay House
1663 Liberty Drive
Bloomington, IN 47403
www.balboapress.com
1 (877) 407-4847

Because of the dynamic nature of the Internet, any web addresses or links contained in this book may have changed since publication and may no longer be valid. The views expressed in this work are solely those of the author and do not necessarily reflect the views of the publisher, and the publisher hereby disclaims any responsibility for them.

The author of this book does not dispense medical advice or prescribe the use of any technique as a form of treatment for physical, emotional, or medical problems without the advice of a physician, either directly or indirectly. The intent of the author is only to offer information of a general nature to help you in your quest for emotional and spiritual well-being. In the event you use any of the information in this book for yourself, which is your constitutional right, the author and the publisher assume no responsibility for your actions.

Any people depicted in stock imagery provided by Thinkstock are models, and such images are being used for illustrative purposes only.
Certain stock imagery © Thinkstock.

Print information available on the last page.

ISBN: 978-1-5043-7542-9 (sc)
ISBN: 978-1-5043-7543-6 (e)

Balboa Press rev. date: 02/28/2017

For Kaliji

TABLE OF CONTENTS

PREFACE

This book is a continuation of a trilogy treating the universal search for liberation. The first book of the trilogy, *Invicti Solis*, addressed the fundamental motivating force of desire, with a secondary interest in psychology, which has in so many ways supplanted religion, theology, and philosophy in our postmodern age. The second book, *The Liberation of Thought*, addressed the role both of Western and Eastern thought in approaching the question of liberation, with a secondary interest in philosophy, religion, and psychology. The third book in the trilogy, *The Sickness of Effort*, addressed the most central of the "skillful means" in spiritual ways or schools: the effort needed to begin the practical struggle for liberation.

The order of the trilogy also represents a progression in pondering the question of identity. In *Invicti Solis* the question of desire is opened and pondered as a way of approaching the deeper question of identity; in *The Liberation of Thought* the different levels and qualities of thought are considered both as obstacles and avenues to liberation; and in *The Sickness of Effort* the question of effort is pondered as the key to transitioning from a bogus identity to an authentic identity.

In tracing this progression in pondering the question of identity, the trilogy also opened the question of how we should best represent to ourselves what we usually consider to be our conventional identity. This identity, what is often called the ego, is an activity, not an entity. What we began to acquire in childhood, and what has been continually reinforced in adolescence and through subsequent developmental stages in adulthood, is a collection of roles that serve to avoid reality.

Initially, in childhood, our precious essence needed protection, and the acquired parts of ourselves, our conditioning, met that need. But over time this conditioning has become not only the protector of our essential nature but also the chief obstacle to it, much as the dragon that guards a hoard of gold in myth and legend. Hence what initially served as a protection against a reality that threatened to overwhelm us has become the unyielding force barring the way to our own inner riches.

We have learned to negotiate with the once threatening outer reality through the instrumentality of our conditioning, through the adoption and gradual refinement of countless roles. The difficulty presented to our wish to continue developing or growing is that the same conditioning blocks ready access to the source of our inner development. The roles we have learned deceive us into believing we have a self and that such a self can act effectively. Both beliefs are false.

Spiritual teachings unite in diagnosing the difficulty but vary widely in how they represent this impediment; they differ in how they communicate this predicament in words, in ideas. One way of representing this state of affairs is to teach that our conventional identity is not one unified 'I' or self but a collection of many 'I's. Many schools of psychology also teach the doctrine of "subpersonalities," that rather than having one personality our conditioning is comprised of many personalities without any unifying center of gravity. This teaching is helpful but not optimal, for it perpetuates the reification of the activity of avoidance.

To prevent the problem of reification, and to highlight the activity that is the ego or socially conditioned feeling of self, it is better to represent this mistaken sense of self and agency as a collection of roles rather than a collection of entities or 'I's. Other, less elevated, attempts to represent this activity have also led to unnecessary quandaries about putative inner entities; one thinks of such ideas as Freud's metapsychology with his positing of *ich*, *es*, and *uberich*, which unfortunately were translated into English as ego, id, and superego, further reinforcing a reification which Freud never intended.

The present book follows up this suggestion by pondering the notion of role playing. Once again psychology, ever parasitic upon spiritual ideas and methods, has taken over the idea of roles and role playing in an attempt to provide therapeutic assistance to those who are prone to seek such help. Yet in so doing psychology fails to address the deeper and more vital questions that naturally occur to one who seeks a liberated condition of being. What clues to this search are revealed in a consideration of the role that roles play in our lives?

Many words are used to name Reality itself: the Absolute, the Source, Awareness itself, the Great Self. Adopting one of these names, we can say that it is the nature of the Source to pour itself out, to empty itself, into manifestation or the created order; this process is variously called involution, emergence, or, as in Christian theology, *kenosis*. And it is also the nature of the Source to return to itself in a process known as evolution. Adopting another of these names, we can also say that the Self, in a process intended to create, maintain, and evolve all manifestation, forgets itself in its embodiment in human beings and, as a necessary part of this process, remembers itself in such an embodiment in order to blend the energies needed to grow the whole.

In its embodiment in human beings, the Self freely adopts the role of an incarnated being, symbolized most dramatically in the incarnation of Jesus as the Christ. Part of the Self in a given man or woman has forgotten itself; another part of the Self, the higher part, has never forgotten and calls to the lower part to remember. The part that has forgotten inhabits the roles played by a given human being.

In learning consciously to play one's many acquired roles, one is in fact remembering the true state of affairs; one is remembering that one's actual Identity is that of the Self, playing the role of a human being playing that being's many acquired roles. The idea of our conditioning as a collection of roles helps in the discovery of this Identity.

Chapter ONE

THE QUESTION OF ROLES

Questions orbiting role playing touch every part of our lives. We intuitively sense that the role we play with our families differs substantially from the role we play at work or with our friends, and yet by and large we feel and sense ourselves to be the same person playing different roles.

This overall feeling is very much like the relationship of an actor or actress to the roles he or she plays in the theatre or in movies. The difference, in contrast to our everyday roles, is that the actor must approach his roles in a professional manner, with far more attention given to preparation and performance. His career depends upon it.

But is it really so different from what is at stake in our daily roles? If we fail to give sufficient attention and care to our roles at work, for example, our professional careers are bound to suffer. People naturally wish to find a family of affiliation in the workplace, and those sharing a work environment usually speak of this association as a family. Yet few of us feel so much at home in this environment that we slip into the more comfortable behaviors we exhibit at home, with our actual families. No matter how welcoming the work setting, there is always the expectation that work related behaviors will be more formal, that is, more professional, than behaviors at home.

The situation with an actress is the same. She is expected to perform as a professional, and behaviors acceptable at home would not be tolerated at work. At home, she is more "herself," while at work she takes on the role of a professional actress. How is this role different from the roles she assumes in a play, a drama or comedy? Presumably the role of an actress is more closely allied to her identity, her sense and feeling of herself, than the roles she assumes in a play. Yet she is also expected to draw upon her own experience, her own sense and feeling of herself, in the preparation for, and performance of, the role of a character in a given play.

While drawing upon his own experience, his own identity, a good actor is expected to remember who he is at all times during the preparation and performance of a role, not to confuse his identity with the role he is playing. An actor who loses himself in an assumed character is not a good actor; in losing himself, in forgetting himself, he has lost the ability to play the role well.

Similarly, in our everyday roles we sense and feel, sometimes intuitively, sometimes more consciously, that who we are, our identity, is distinct from the role we play. This distinction is most apparent in our work setting; while at work we are usually more aware that we must adopt certain behaviors and attitudes that usually do not obtain in other settings, and because our careers and thus our livelihoods depend upon such performance-oriented behaviors, we are more alert to role playing in work settings than in most other cultural environments.

Another setting in which role playing is paramount is in a religious or spiritual setting. Again, behaviors which are acceptable at home would not be tolerated in a setting devoted to worship or spiritual development. Although role playing is necessary in spiritual environments, it is more subtle than in work settings because of the delicacy and nobility of spiritual endeavors. People in such a setting can be hypersensitive to an overt display of religiosity, and behaviors rewarded in the workplace will be punished in a spiritual setting, often accompanied by cries of "hypocrite." In a spiritual setting playing a role is complicated not only by the subtlety required but also by the greater participation of one's identity in the role.

Here the similarity with the acting profession is far more obvious than role playing in a work setting. Although the actress has to play a role *as* an actress in that work setting, she also has to invest far more of her identity in her *character* roles than that expected in most other work environments. Her role as an actress is not that different than any other work-related role, but her role as a character in a play for theater or screen is strikingly similar to that demanded of one in a spiritual setting—in particular a spiritual leader such as a pastor, priest, rabbi, or imam.

In an exoteric spiritual setting it is above all the spiritual leader or mentor who must invest his identity in his spiritual role, much as an actor must invest his identity in his character role. In an esoteric spiritual setting all participants feel the pressure to invest an equal portion of their identities in a collective attempt to develop spiritually. To be sure, elders or leaders in an esoteric group or school must set a standard or example, but every member of the school shares equal responsibility for investment of identity in the role assumed in the school.

Why this similarity between identity investment in the acting profession and spiritual settings? In the acting profession the performer must draw heavily upon his experience in order to play a given character role authentically, that is, with real feeling, and for this to occur the actor must invest his own sense and feeling of himself, his identity, into the role of the character he is portraying. In a religious or spiritual setting, the dynamic is the same: the individual in such a setting feels the need to play a role as a member of the spiritual community; this role is analogous to the role an actor plays as an actor, and does not require much in the way of identity investment. Like an actor, such an individual enters a period of preparation, an initiation into what will eventually become a questioning of identity itself.

A good actor is not prepared to leap into a character role; he needs an extensive period of preparation during which he trains his attention, relaxes his tensions, and practices various somatic disciplines like movements. In approaching the role he is to play, he questions his own identity, not radically but just enough to be able to play the part authentically.

A similar dynamic obtains in a spiritual setting. In exoteric spiritual communities, in typical churches for example, the demand for identity investment varies widely. Some exoteric communities demand very little, not much more than the initial playing of a role in the group, more demanding and subtle than in a work setting, but not calling upon much identity investment. Other exoteric settings, by contrast, urge a given individual to invest far more identity beyond that initially required; such groupings encourage participants to examine themselves seriously by a standard that calls for some questioning of one's identity, one's usual sense and feeling of oneself.

An authentic esoteric spiritual group or school is most like the dynamic that obtains in a school of acting. Initially a participant is required to play a role as a new member of the school; for this role little identity investment is needed. Right away, however, ideas and practices are introduced that demand that the aspirant begin to question her usual sense and feeling of herself, her identity. In order to develop spiritually this questioning must deepen, so much so that one's identity begins to reveal itself as a collection of roles that one plays depending upon the setting in which one finds oneself.

Obviously this is a more radical questioning of identity than that which obtains in a school of acting. A good actress questions her identity in order to play a character role well; a good aspirant in a spiritual school questions her identity in order to develop an authentic Identity and in so doing reveal the inauthentic identity as a collection of roles developed originally in childhood and refined through further development into adolescence and finally adulthood.

The real Identity, discovered in a spiritual school, is analogous to the conventional identity of the actor, and the collection of roles that comprises the conventional identity of one in a spiritual school is analogous to the varied character roles assumed by an actor. In the acting school, one is counseled never to forget one's conventional identity while playing a character role; in a spiritual school, one is counseled never to forget one's real Identity while playing the varied roles that comprise one's conventional identity. This counsel, however, is very difficult to follow.

Because of this difficulty, and because the analogy of role playing is so powerful in its ability to evoke feeling, the observation and study of the acting profession offers the promise of considerable help in understanding the roles that comprise our conventional identity and how such roles may be played more consciously with an awareness of an always available Identity or real Self acting as the Source and Condition of all conditions. And there is more, so much more, at stake.

Our conventional identities, the roles we play, are bids for immortality, a denial of death, of limitation. In this regard acting itself, acting on the stage or screen, is a bid for immortality. But death will not be denied; we are limited, mortal, if by "we" is meant our conventional identities supported by our somatic structure—all subject to death. All cultural forms, all roles played in societies of whatever complexity or simplicity, are heroic narratives designed to avoid reality, avoid what is here and now, and, eventually, intended to avoid the end of all roles.

Training as an actor or actress is meant to play a character role authentically, in the moment, with real feeling. While always remembering one's conventional identity, one plays a role consciously. Training in an esoteric school is likewise learning to play one's conventional roles authentically, always remembering one's real Identity, understanding that the usual way of playing roles is above all an activity of avoidance, avoiding reality, avoiding Being, avoiding the inevitable end of such "activity," avoiding death.

The conventional playing of a role is a futile "activity," futile because reality cannot be avoided. And yet we are always trying to avoid it, always trying to avoid "what is." We would rather be anywhere but here, and at any other time than now. Such is the function, the purpose and meaning, informing conventional role playing, one's conventional identity. It is intended above all to avoid Being, Reality, what is.

And yet, ironically, it is a bid for Being, for immortality, for imperishable life. All our so-called activity, all our role playing, is a search for Being, for Truth, for Eternity. And it is futile because it is a search based in ignorance of the meaning and purpose of life itself. What is needed is knowledge; just as the actor or actress must acquire knowledge in a school of acting, so we must acquire knowledge in a school of Being.

Studying an actor's training to inhabit a role authentically can yield intellectual knowledge of how to inhabit our own roles authentically. But real knowledge is a gift from above, and can only be obtained by removing the obstacles that prevent its lawful descent: the futile activity of unexamined role playing.

So what is at stake in such a study? What is at stake in being able to receive a knowledge without quotation marks? What is at stake is a transcendence of death; what is at stake is immortality.

Chapter TWO

LIFE AT THE LIMITS

Existentialism

Existentialism is a philosophical movement that saw its best days subsequent to World War II, popularized by Jean Paul Sartre, and which began to decline in popularity after the 1960s. In its heyday it galvanized disaffected youth in particular, and compared to it all other philosophical movements seemed, particularly to nonphilosophers, arid, remote from life. Indeed, many felt that most philosophy was little more than a distraction from life itself.

What appealed to so many young people of the time was that existentialism began its philosophical thought with extreme situations encountered in life rather than with abstract propositions far removed from life's vitality. The subject matter of existentialist thought was the plight of humans in extremity, facing despair, destitution, derangement, deprivation, death, and so on. Such thought took the form not only of philosophical books and essays but also in plays, novels, short stories, poems, paintings, and sculpture. Sartre and Camus in particular were prolific existentialist literary figures. During the 1960s a growing social conscience concerned with oppression and injustice among young people helped spread existentialist ideas, which usually included these concerns.

A Brief History Of Philosophy

A relevant history of philosophy helps to account for the emergence of existential thought. Greek pre-Socratic thought initiated Western philosophy as we know it, and their concerns were with apparent abstractions like being and becoming. When we come to later developments, to Socrates, Plato, and Aristotle, it becomes more apparent that being and becoming were not mere abstractions of thought to these thinkers, but were also sought as living realities in the schools of self-development that they founded, the Academy of Plato and the Lyceum of Aristotle.

Therefore during this period of ancient philosophy, including later Greek and Roman thought, ideas were not pondered for their own sake but were catalysts for the development of being. Philosophy was not in any sense a distraction from life but an invitation to a deeper immersion in life, including its less pleasant features. Intensity was sought no less than serenity; in fact, the aim of a philosophical school was the concomitant increase of both these elements of life: an intense immersion in experience, including extreme situations, and a serene oversight to all experience, whether extreme or commonplace.

After this classical period medieval philosophy became the obedient handmaiden of Christian theology in Europe. Thought itself became more abstract, less interested in life, as it supported a theological interest in another world. Development of being was by and large confined to monastic enclaves, while the earliest universities became more and more academic, less and less interested in the reality of being.

The overall tone for modern philosophy was set by Descartes; being a superb mathematician, he wanted to make philosophy in the image of science, itself guided by mathematics. The certainty sought by Descartes was not the certainty sought by Plato; the latter sought the certainty of being, while the former sought the certainty of abstract thought. Subsequent philosophers continued this quest, which culminated in Kant's insistence that we can be certain only of abstract thought, by which we experience the world.

Schopenhauer accepted Kant's dictum but was the first Western thinker of note to be touched to the core by Eastern thought, particularly Buddhism. This influence introduced into Western thought a profound concern for suffering and for extreme human conditions. Kierkegaard, who did not consider himself a philosopher, nevertheless came to be regarded as the first real existential thinker; he wrote several books about such extreme states of mind like despair, which he called the "sickness unto death." And Nietzsche, under Schopenhauer's influence, also wrote about humanity's extremity and how art can transfigure terror into beauty. The latter view Nietzsche derived from his interpretation of Greek tragedy, not from Schopenhauer.

Kierkegaard and Nietzsche most influenced modern existential thought, yet neither they nor the thinkers that followed them fathomed the intense immersion in life so characteristic of ancient philosophy; all they saw was the serenity, in particular the serenity of Socrates on full display in Plato's *Apology*. Whatever "serenity" remained with philosophy was an academic phenomenon removed from the exigencies of life. The legacy of Descartes and Kant issued in such modern philosophical schools as positivism, analytic philosophy, symbolic logic, phenomenology, structuralism, poststructuralism, and semiotics. All such schools were regarded by existentialists as distractions from real living.

The Birth Of Arid Thought From Greek Tragedy

In his first book, *The Birth of Tragedy*, Nietzsche argued that the intense concern with extremity staged by Greek tragedians died when Euripides began to introduce argument or dialectic into the speeches of his characters. Debate about conflict began to replace concern with conflict itself, which in its turn produced a Plato whose art form was a dialogue between interlocutors, a verbal contest that focused exclusively on coming to correct, abstract conclusions.

Nietzsche also pointed to Aristotle's *Poetics*, in which the latter argued that the tragic hero must be deficient in virtue in order for tragedy to occur, as a further example of how an intense interest in extreme situations died. For Aristotle, virtue entailed serenity, along with a strong inclination to dialogue one's way to a compromise agreement among combatants, thus avoiding tragedy. What Nietzsche failed to see was how that serenity, for Aristotle, is compatible with, and indeed impossible without, the most profound intensity and engagement with life.

Thus a tragic hero like Oedipus, for example, while outstanding in passionate intensity, is not outstanding in virtue, lacking serenity. For intensity without serenity is a curse and a deficiency, and may, given unfavorable circumstances, lead to a tragic outcome. At the same time, the example of Socrates shows that even an individual outstanding in virtue may come to an unfavorable end. Aristotle does not consider such an individual's unlucky demise tragic but rather shocking, and so not good material for a tragic performance on stage. The injustice of such an end for one with outstanding virtue is, for Aristotle, too great; it shocks rather than elicits the tragic emotions of ruth and terror.

That the tragic poets Aeschylus, Sophocles, and Euripides staged immense suffering that elicited "pity" or ruth and terror from the audience there is no doubt. And that they were above all concerned with life's extremities is also beyond question. There was not, however, a gradual rationalization of life from Aeschylus to Euripides as Nietzsche argues; indeed, it is in Aeschylus more than any other tragedian that we find a condemnation of passionate abandon and a strong approval of reason and compromise, thereby attaining justice and avoiding tragedy. And it was Hegel who argued that the focus of tragedy is not the tragic hero but an avoidable tragic conflict between antagonists, and the lack of virtue reveals itself in a stubborn insistence by a character in the drama on having his own way. While outstanding in his honesty, Oedipus is heedless in insisting on discovering the truth, putting at risk not just himself and others but the entire community. He ignores the warnings of the seer or prophet and when he finally discovers the truth blinds and exiles himself.

The Philosophy Of Stage And Screen

Thus one can see that existentialism is the philosophy most on display on stage and screen. Even playwrights who wish to press a social or political agenda, like Brecht and Shaw, must utilize the drama of extremity to deliver their message.

Rooted in Greek tragedy and comedy, subsequent developments in theater productions and, much later, in film, embody an overarching concern with suffering, tragic collision, and the possible character development that such events produce. Although the Greek tragedians produced original material, the phenomenon of Greek drama was itself rooted in Homer's *Iliad*, its myth and spiritual dimension, as well as in the "spirit of music," as Nietzsche maintained. The chorus, ever present, passes judgment upon characters and events.

The Spiritual Dimension

Homer's epic has an emphatic spiritual dimension in the parts the gods play in the affairs of men and women. When Achilles gives way to wrath Homer explains it is due to a god acting upon him. Changes in behavior in a character are not due to individual development but rather to the differing whims of various gods and goddesses. In this regard gods are intimately involved in producing extreme situations.

Eastern spirituality is also most concerned with extreme situations; the best example is the teaching of the Buddha. He taught that men and women are subject to old age, sickness, and death, and that such extremities call for extreme measures. Spiritual or wisdom teachings, East or West, are all addressing the fact of extremity, in particular the facts of limitation and death. Such teachings offer remedies to these facts, in one way or another offering a way out, beyond limitation and death.

Life At The Limits

Thus life at the limits can be taken in two ways: one is the way of existentialism, facing the limitations of life with the sort of courage that allows one to begin living beyond despair, as Sartre put it; the other is the way of spirituality, conquering despair by living beyond the limitations of time and death, in eternity. The first affirms intensity; the second reconciles intensity and serenity. The first beckons the actor of stage and screen; the second beckons the actor in life.

Philosophy's Objection To Poetics

The Greeks understood philosophy to be the search for wisdom, and in their schools activities were provided to assist that search. A philosophical school did not exist to arrive at correct conclusions about reality; it existed to recognize and incorporate reality. The most well known and long lasting of these schools was Plato's Academy.

Plato is famous for his objections to poetics generally, and especially to the staging of extreme situations. He felt that it would glorify a life of intensity and lead many astray, including some promising students of philosophy. Aristotle believed that staged plays were not harmful so long as they purged audiences of emotion and inclined them to the contemplative, or philosophical, life. Plato did not believe that watching a man or woman of "middling" virtue come to grief was at all conducive to seeking wisdom, while Aristotle thought such dramas would teach the need for such a search.

The divide in modern philosophy between existentialism and approaches like language analysis came about because philosophy lost its reason for being: being itself. One half of the original philosophical impulse was retained while the other half—the most important one— was forgotten. What was retained was the impulse to attain clarity and reach correct conclusions through argument; what was lost was the impulse to further spiritual development, the development of one's being. Hence both existentialism and analytic philosophy are crippled as they search not for wisdom, not for being, but for correct "philosophical" conclusions in thought, what Plato called "opinion."

The interest in the intensity of extreme experiences was rediscovered by philosophers through encounters with Eastern wisdom and Greek tragedy. These discoveries, along with first hand experiences in Europe during and after two World Wars, launched existentialism as a philosophical movement. Analytic philosophy was a continuation of the interest in attaining a measure of knowledge or certainty, first about reality, then, after Kant, about concepts or language, the uses of language. Both sides of the philosophical divide failed to understand an authentic search for wisdom, leading to a reconciliation between intensity and serenity. As concepts, they cannot be reconciled; they can only be reconciled through total conceptual surrender to Being itself.

Existentialism And The Theater

As the philosophy of intensity, of extremity, of in effect drama, existentialism was bound to have a profound effect upon playwrights, directors, and actors. More than any other philosophy it came to dominate stage and screen, more than Brecht's Marxism or Shaw's Fabian Socialism. For even in the cases of these two men, the extreme events of drama played a dominant role over any political agenda. Audiences were not moved by ideology but by the action on stage or screen.

Such dominance, of course, also obtained in the training and performances of actors and actresses as well as in the acting schools that taught them how to act a role with authenticity. Theories of acting such as Stanislavski's were steeped in existential thought, and even more so the theories of men like Grotowski and Brook. We will explore the far reaching effects of this philosophy on the theater in the next chapter.

Chapter THREE
THE EXISTENTIAL ACTOR

The Existential Nihilist

Most existentialists, with some exceptions, are nihilists not in the sense that they find no meaning in themselves but that they find no meaning in the cosmos, the universe. For them, the universe is a meaningless movement of material and energy, without any overarching purpose. Any meaning must be supplied by us, and the mistake made by most pre-existential thinkers and actors is that they mistook their projections of meaning as inherent in the universe.

Sartre, the man who most popularized existentialism, is a prime example of this view. For Sartre the world is without meaning; discovering this fact leads to despair, and the philosopher or artist must then create meaning from himself. Thus, for Sartre, "life begins on the other side of despair."

The Denial Of Death

Ernest Becker wrote a very influential book in the early 1970s that further popularized this view, *The Denial of Death*. In that book Becker argues that human character, a sense of identity, develops as a "vital lie," a life and death project that serves to give meaning to an otherwise meaningless existence and that, above all, denies the reality of death and finitude by becoming a bid for immortality, an "immortality project."

Becker maintained that this was an "impossible" project, impossible but necessary: impossible, because it flies in the face of the reality of death and meaninglessness; necessary, because without it we would not only fall into dread and despair but also be unable to move beyond them, as Sartre insisted we must.

Human Character As A Collection Of Roles

The vital lie that is human character, the immortality project that shields us from death and gives meaning to our lives, is a collection of roles. The first role we learn is the part we play in our family of origin: some play the part of the hero, while others play the lost child or the rebel. There are many roles in a given family system, and in order for the system to remain in balance each family member must not vary substantially from the role that member has been assigned. To a greater or lesser degree this initial role is carried forward into all subsequent settings and informs all subsequent roles. And it is the role with which we most identify, that comes closest to determining who we think we are, our identity.

As the settings we are in begin to multiply, new roles are developed, grown organically out of the initial family role. In school the hero tends to shine academically, while the rebel tends to be an underachiever while taking an oppositional attitude toward authority figures. These are tendencies only, and it is impossible to predict how a given individual will develop; a rebel, for example, may find meaning in refusing to become a doctor like mother and father wants and instead shine as an English professor in her course of development. In one way or another the initial role *tends* to inform all subsequent roles.

In work settings a rebel faces difficulties that the hero usually evades. For both, success in work depends upon developing a functional work role. The rebel has to learn to work around authority while the hero must learn to restrain his inclination to outshine everyone, including those that exercise executive power. Given enough time, an individual may be able to be more "herself," that is, include more of her initial family role in her work role, and when this further inclusion occurs she will be more likely to identify herself with her role in the workplace; she will invest more of her identity in that role.

Notice what has happened. What *is* her identity? It is her familial role. I will argue later that it is a bogus identity, but for now I will maintain that her identity is how she feels herself to be, and that her identity is a collection of thoughts, feelings, sensations, and actions that she learned as a child, further developed in school and early work experiences; it is an *activity*, not an entity, and we often use a shorthand name for it called the ego, a sense and feeling of herself. And this activity is the role she learned to play in her family of origin. In becoming more comfortable in her work setting she feels safe enough to invest more of what she considers herself in her work role. In this way so many people become identified with their career or their profession: they invest their identity in their professional role.

The Existential Actor

So we come to the profession of acting. A given actor or actress brings to his profession his most intimate familial role, further shaped and tempered by school and perhaps other work settings. The profession of acting is of extraordinary interest in that it demands that the actor play different roles in order to advance his career. Yet most actors are so identified with their familial roles that they believe it is their real self, their real identity.

In acting school actors are told they must invest themselves in their character roles; they are asked to question themselves, question their identity, but not radically; they are to question themselves just enough to play a given role authentically, with feeling. In so doing they come to conceive of themselves as existential actors.

Life Or Death

For the existential actor acting is a life or death proposition. Jeff Zinn, for example, accepts Becker's diagnosis of the human condition and maintains that because audiences intuitively sense their condition, the condition from which they try to escape with their own immortality projects, any staged play that does not dramatize this life or death question will fail to engage them; they will turn away, sensing that the play and so the playwright are not serious.

Acting is a life or death affair not just because of the audience; for the actor, playing a role on stage requires a temporary relaxation of his own usual role, just enough to be able to "surrender" to the requirements of the assumed character in a play. Because our usual role provides a kind of "character armor" against meaninglessness and death, it is a very risky affair to question, relax, and search within it for the somatic and emotional resources needed to play a part authentically.

Surrender

The act of surrender, so essential in the acting profession, is also essential in a spiritual search. The analogy is exact: the actor's surrender of his usual identity is analogous to the seeker's surrender of her usual identity, and the actor's assumption of a part in a play is analogous to a seeker's assumption of a role in life. The essential ingredient in both is awareness or consciousness.

The actor's profession demands an increase in awareness not common in most work roles. The demand is extended to a searching critique of oneself, not radical as in spiritual seekers, but far more daunting than anything found in usual professional life. Of course such a critique can be found in other work settings, particularly in preparation stages. But usually such self-examination is required only once, even if over an extended period of time, whereas for the actor it must be undergone whenever a new role is assumed.

In learning the intentions of the assumed character in a play, the actor must search his own experiences and, when needed, imagine what it must be like to be that character, what Stanislavski called the magical "what if." The actor may not realize that when conducting such a search he is coming perilously close to questioning his identity in a radical way, precisely the way a spiritual seeker conducts her own self-inquiry. Usually the actor manages to investigate his experience without a radical outcome, but often those in the acting profession, including directors and playwrights, also become spiritual seekers. Two notable individuals are Peter Brook and Jerzy Grotowski.

Awareness Of Self

Another demand placed upon the existential actor, once the assumed role is learned and his emotional resources are marshaled, is never to forget one's self while acting, to always be aware that one is not the role one is playing. The demand is there because it is all too easy to forget one's self.

Aspirants in authentic spiritual ways or paths learn right away that they almost always forget themselves. They enter a spiritual way implicitly believing the opposite: that they always remember themselves. It is an implicit belief because until an elder in a given way directs their attention to this belief they usually never think about it. Once they become convinced that they indeed almost always forget themselves, the demand to remember themselves takes on supreme importance if they wish to continue on that way of inner development.

The counsel that an actor remember himself is far less demanding; it amounts to an admonition that his work as an actor will suffer if he confuses his identity with the role he is portraying on stage. An increase in awareness or consciousness is required in order to sustain this distinction. Otherwise it would be too easy to lose oneself in one's role. And in losing oneself, one loses the ability to act well. In becoming the assumed character so thoroughly, one ceases to be an actor.

An exact parallel obtains in spiritual ways or paths. The demand to remember oneself is a demand not to lose oneself in one's roles, in particular the primordial, familial role. A given aspirant comes to realize that she is continually losing herself in her roles in life, that her roles have become her identity, a false identity that needs to be questioned at every moment. How can this questioning be sustained? By recognizing one's roles *as* roles, as parts one is playing in order to negotiate skillfully with life, and in so doing not confuse them with one's real identity, just as an actor, in recognizing his assumed role as a role, cannot confuse that role with what he conceives, erroneously, to be his real identity. The actor comes very near to discovering the truth, but usually avoids going deep enough to engage a spiritual search.

Shape

Zinn, in his book *The Existential Actor*, defines shape as how we form our immortality projects, including how we present ourselves on the outside and how we conceive ourselves on the inside. Also included in this "shape" are our motivations, what we want in life. Obviously the existential actor, like the rest of us, wants to matter, to inject some meaning into his life, to create a meaningful career in the acting profession within an overarching life that amounts to a symbolic kind of immortality.

Upon entering the acting profession or an acting school, one's motivations take on more substantial "shape" as the demands of the school become more apparent. In addition to wanting to matter in a general sense one also comes to want to matter in learning to be an accomplished actor. We have already discussed several of these demands, and the budding actor wishes to meet them so that current and future transactions with elders and peers will issue in professional performances on stage.

Similarly, an aspirant in a spiritual school is motivated to matter, and such a one has often concluded that the varied roles in life, including professional roles, are insufficient to matter in a cosmic sense. Unlike most existentialists, such an aspirant intuitively feels that meaning is inherent in the cosmos, and that one's motivations somehow correspond to that meaning. Upon entering a school of inner work, one's motivations take on more definite shape as one first learns the intellectual ideas presented for one's consideration and then follows the elders' suggestions to verify those ideas in one's inner laboratory. In order to develop inwardly, one learns to act outwardly; even one's new role in the school is treated as an assumed role, much as an actor assumes a role in a play. Questioning one's usual identity, one finds it to be a collection of roles orbiting one's familial role, and with which one has mistakenly identified. Perhaps the school uses the analogy of professional acting to assist in the transition from a bogus sense of identity to a recognition of a real Identity. Just as an actor learns to distinguish himself from his roles, so one learns to distinguish one's authentic Identity from the roles one assumes in life.

Transactions

Zinn continues his discussion of what he considers to be the essential elements in an existential actor's quiver by referring to what acting schools call transactions, usually interactions between actors but also, for example in Grotowski's theatrical theory, transactions between actor and audience.

Some acting schools emphasize interactions between actors, for example in the Meisner repetition exercises and in the dramatic theory of David Mamet. In ordinary life, we continually find ourselves measuring the appropriateness or efficacy of our behavior with others by the validation or lack thereof that we receive from them. Similarly, the actor must measure the efficacy of his performance by the interactions that obtain with other actors and the audience.

Theorists who place transactions at the heart of acting maintain that too much attention and so emphasis is placed on emotion or the emotional memory in more traditional acting schools, and that by moving transactions with others to center stage one removes the need to conjure the appropriate emotion; the emotion, they argue, will arise with the right transaction, that is, the right action.

Action

Another essential feature of the existential actor is right action. Action follows organically from shape, from our motivations to obtain what we want. Once an actor determines what an assumed character wants, the appropriate action will follow.

Existential thinkers like Sartre also put more emphasis on action, on what we do, in the often quoted "existence precedes essence." That is, our being or character is formed by our actions, and so being develops according to our activity. In that sense the superlative German man of letters Goethe is the exemplar and forerunner: he taught that we define ourselves by our actions, by our endeavors and creations, and he actually denied that we have any such thing as essence or a soul, a self. We *are* what we *do*.

The existential actor will therefore place primacy upon action, upon what he does on the stage. Every such action has an intention, an objective. Usually, especially in drama, there are obstacles to overcome in order to attain the objective. And of course there are motivations; the assumed character in a play wishes to attain something, is motivated to exert sufficient effort to obtain what he desires. All these internal dynamics figure into the outer action.

The contrast with spiritual or wisdom teachings could not be more dramatic. For Sartre and other existentialists, the fact that a man or woman simply *is* is not sufficient; in order to attain sufficiency, in order to become essential in a truly human sense, a man or woman must *do*, must create, must take action, must act. In a given wisdom tradition, a man or woman must act as he or she has learned to act, only, with time, to find that such action is not true action at all. And in the process of learning this difficult truth, he or she also learns the meaning of his or her Being, that *isness* is indeed sufficient apart from any putative action. I will explore this important question in more depth later in the book, for it is an essential element in studying the role of role playing in life.

Chapter FOUR
AN ACTOR PREPARES

Relevance

Not all of an actor's preparation is relevant to our study, but much of it is. Stanislavski divided an actor's preparation into two parts: work on the self, and work on the role. The preparation most relevant to the question of role playing in ordinary life is work on the self.

Yet even within work on the self not all preparation for playing a role on stage is relevant, the primary example being vocal training. Exercises are given to train the entire vocal apparatus until it becomes second nature, until the actor no longer has to think about doing such things as supporting the breath and placing the voice in what voice teachers call "the mask," in the bones of the face, in order to attain appropriate resonance. Sources are provided in the bibliography for those who are interested in pursuing voice training, but such exercises, like work on a given role, are not pertinent to the question we are pondering.

Stanislavski

The source of most preparatory ideas in acting schools is Constantin Stanislavski, the Russian actor, director, and teacher who formulated a very complex system of training that has proven to be unwieldy in practice but which has continued to provide inspiration for generations of actors, directors, and acting teachers. In his teaching method Stanislavski addressed such important preparatory elements as attention, relaxation, movement, the process of self-study, the life of the body, the creation of a soul, emotional memory, physical actions, remembering oneself on stage, avoiding acting for results, connecting different centers in the body, motivations-intentions-objectives, and a feeling for truth. In addressing how an actor prepares we will address several of these elements.

Concentration Of Attention

Anyone who has ever taught any sort of a subject understands through experience how fragile and even fickle our power of attention is. Even students who are gifted constantly drift from the topic, usually indulging in daydreams or other flights of undirected attention such as following a chain of associative thoughts.

In the acting profession, the most deadly drifting of one's attention occurs when one is distracted by the audience. Stanislavski taught that in order to prevent such distraction one must learn to concentrate one's attention upon something or someone on the stage. He appealed to attracted attention in insisting that one must take an active interest in this object or fellow actor. For training the attention he created several exercises.

One such exercise involved leaving the entire auditorium and stage dark, with only one object on the stage highlighted with a bright spotlight. Acting students were told to concentrate their attention upon that object for a period of time. Because it was the only object that could be seen, students found that it could be easily found again if their attention drifted.

Next the spotlight was widened a bit, so that not only the chosen object was lit but also a space of a few feet around it. This time the demand to concentrate on the object was more difficult, for not only could the attention wander from the one and only object highlighted but also it could wander from that object to another object on stage that was now also highlighted. Once again the spotlight was widened, so that now much more of the stage was lit; the student had to keep concentrating on the chosen object, and once more the task was found to be more difficult than the previous two exercises.

Finally the entire stage was lit, and for the third time the students were required to concentrate upon the one object that had originally been lit. Finding that this task was the hardest of all, the students realized that the more objects in their field of vision the more difficult it would be to remain concentrating on one object. At this point the topic of interest was often introduced, indicating that an attracted attention is more able to hold one's interest than a directed attention alone.

At the same time, however, directed attention was essential. The intention to direct one's attention, then, could be strengthened with attracted attention if the object or person was interesting enough. The more attractive the object, said Stanislavski, the more the attention will be concentrated.

His students also found that they did not understand the effort needed to concentrate; usually, when told to focus their attention on an object, they bore down hard, made a tremendous effort to "really see" the object, and in so doing tensed the muscles of their face, neck, and shoulders. Less is more, Stanislavski would say; less effort is more concentration. Students would be guided into seeing a given object with far less effort than they imagined possible, with far more relaxation than thought possible.

Relaxation Of Muscles

The above example is only one among many exercises given to acting students to train them to relax the muscles of their bodies. Freeing the body from unnecessary tension was taught as being absolutely essential to prepare for an acting career; actors who fail to learn how to relax while on stage will invariably sabotage their chances of acting naturally and with feeling. The voice falters and movements become stiff and maladroit.

Students were taught that they must practice muscle relaxation constantly, whether on stage or in ordinary life. When they asked how this could possibly be done, Stanislavski told them they must develop an observer or "controller," an inner attentiveness that could observe the state of their bodies and allow relaxation to occur naturally. He taught that though it is impossible to eliminate all tension, it is possible, with sufficient self-observation, to accept what tension there is and thereby allow the natural process of relaxation to occur. Forcing the body to relax will create more tension, not less; trusting that the body will relax when attended and accepted will produce the desired result.

Developing A Sense Of Truth

Stanislavski taught that in order to develop a sense of truth on the stage one must believe sincerely in the actions in which one is engaged. And for this development to manifest in a convincing performance one must continue and deepen self-observation, what he called "self-study."

Stress was placed upon being convinced of the truth of one's actions and emotions on stage; without such conviction one's fellow performers and the audience will not be persuaded to believe in one's role. In order to inhabit a role with such conviction, the actor has to believe in the part and in his ability to play it. That task is not as simple or easy as it may sound.

First there are the lingering doubts about whether one is really up to playing the part; then there are doubts and fears about whether the audience and one's fellow performers will find one's performance convincing. These doubts, and others like them, can be overcome only through a thoroughgoing self-examination, including the daily self-observation needed to know oneself deeply.

In working toward a sense or conviction of truth, physical actions on stage must be believable, to the actor, his peers, and the audience. Attentiveness to the coherence of actions is paramount; they must be performed exactly as they would be in life. Once the actor attains the right amount of physical detail, a growing conviction of belief in the action will assist in becoming more comfortable with the role, feeling confident that one's fellow actors and the audience will also accept the acting as believable.

Physical Actions

The physical actions one performs on stage, done correctly and with sufficient realism, have an indispensable influence upon the emotions. By placing primary importance upon the realistic performance of physical actions, the actor no longer need be concerned about generating the correct emotion for the part; the emotion will flow organically from the action.

Thus Stanislavski advised his students to place their entire attention upon what they must do on stage, on the action that needed performing, rather than on their emotions. In so doing emotions would be influenced indirectly, rather than attempting a direct approach to them. Although Stanislavski taught using one's emotional memory to recall past emotional experience as a way to help imagine how a character feels, Meisner, one his students, said that toward the end of his life Stanislavski abandoned this suggestion in favor of the primacy of physical actions. The best way to imagine how a character would feel and also evoke that emotion in oneself is to engage in believable actions.

This method is required, maintained Stanislavski, because there is no way to access emotion directly, guaranteeing that when the moment comes on stage one will be able to generate it. And if one does try to emote directly, placing that inner activity before one's outer activity, one will tend to "tear it to tatters," to dramatize emotion in a way that is unconvincing to all, including the actor. What results is a species of "mechanical acting."

Maintaining an unbroken thread or continuity of the part of the role one is playing is called "the life of the body." Neither on nor off the stage should this thread be broken; if one exits the stage, forgets the role to be "oneself" again, and then reenters later in the play, one risks losing the thread of action entirely. What Stanislavski calls "the creation of the soul" in the part happens of itself once a believable thread of action is created and maintained throughout, for action and feeling, the body and the soul, are connected, for Stanislavski; for him the connection of body and soul amounts to a connection between action and feeling.

Remember Yourself

Stanislavski insisted that an actor should never forget himself while on stage by losing himself in the part. Far from being someone else, in portraying a character one must above all be himself, never forgetting who he is.

Another way of putting this rule is that an actor can never get away from himself, and to avoid false or artificial acting one must draw upon one's own emotional resources in playing a part authentically. Of course one must imagine oneself to be different in myriad ways, but fundamentally one is using one's own inner life, and if a given part is too far removed from one's inner life it should be excluded from one's repertory.

The playwright creates the character in the script; the actor creates the part. In bringing his imagination, his feelings, his experience, to the part, he only brings himself; he cannot materialize the playwright's character out of thin air, creating *ex nihilo* another inner life; he must bring his own life experience in order to breathe life into the written part. There is no other way. And for that he must "remember" himself.

Evidently Stanislavski thought it was possible so to lose oneself in a role that an actor could forget he was acting. What he did not seem to understand is that is precisely what we are doing almost all the time: losing ourselves in our roles.

Results

It is natural to desire favorable outcomes or results in any creative endeavor, and so it is in the acting profession. All actors want to do well, to attain a measure of artistic satisfaction, and to please peers and audience. But according to Stanislavski working for results is inadvisable.

An actor is tempted to reduplicate a success, a performance that went well and garnered much applause. "Never begin with results," Stanislavski advised, and added that the proper results will come if one attends the causes of the favorable outcome rather than focusing on repeating it. Here again is the futile attempt to influence emotion directly rather than what causes it: the realistic, believable physical action.

Harmonious Acting

For Stanislavski there are three movers or motive forces in our psychic lives: mind, feelings, and will. These three, so likely to function separately, must be in harmony. The question for Stanislavski's students, then, is how this can occur.

His students have already learned that feelings cannot be approached directly, and for Stanislavski will is equated with desire, or wish. One begins with an artistic wish to approach a role with the mind, to understand it, interpret it, as much as possible before beginning to act it out. But for maximum efficacy, and to bring the three motive forces into harmony, a "fascinating objective" that requires an unbroken, coherent line of physical actions to attain must predominate.

In other words, there must be an aim, an aim attractive enough to elicit actions and so evoke feeling. From feeling will come the emotional force to harmonize the motive forces; from a clear cut objective comes a clear, unified, creative state.

Connecting Head And Heart

Stanislavski also taught the importance of self-communion, being related to oneself in such a way that head and heart would be connected. He knew about the concept of *prana*, an energetic life force that he believed was Hindu in origin, and that through access to this force a more unified state of being could be produced.

He told his students that while the West is familiar with the functioning of the brain and its executive rule, what was less familiar was the Eastern notion of the life force centered in the solar plexus, near the heart. For self-communion, for a more unified state of being, one needs to connect these two centers, the head and the heart.

The purpose of this connection is to find a way to commune with oneself, to find a subject and an object of communication. For Stanislavski the head is the subject and the heart the object. On stage one can thus commune with oneself while in action. He thought this communion was an essential part of keeping one's attention on stage rather than have it distracted by the audience, if necessary creating a "fourth wall" between the stage and the footlights.

Movements

Equally important in one's preparation as an actor or actress is a study of movement, including body alignment, different forms of dance, movement technologies, and attention given to movement – a subset of physical action – on the stage. Movement technologies recommended for actors have included the Laban system, the Lecoq system, the Alexander technique, the Feldenkrais method, and the Rosen method. We will examine only two of these technologies.

F. Matthais Alexander created the Alexander technique, a way of freeing and balancing the body as well as establishing a more grounded sense of alignment. The playwright Bernard Shaw recommended the training for his actors and participated in its execution himself. It is the most widely known and used movement technology in the acting profession. It is conducted both in supine and standing positions; when supine, the student is instructed to become aware of somatic tensions, allowing them to relax simply through becoming aware of them; when standing, work on correct spinal alignment is conducted. The Alexander technique is used not only for actors but also for dancers and singers.

Moshe Feldenkrais formulated and taught the Feldenkrais method, a way to attain awareness of one's self through the body. The focus tends to be not only on the body's soft tissue but also the skeletal system. To promote better awareness of the body much of the work is done in a supine position. One exercise intended to free the neck and jaw is to move one's head slowly from side to side, gently and never forcing, while imagining there is a very long feather attached to one's nose and, as the head moves, one is touching the ceiling with the feather. Many actors utilize this method of body awareness work; Feldenkrais himself worked with Peter Brook's company of actors, helping them free their jaws and breathe more naturally.

Preparatory Elements

Later in the book I will be exploring in depth the preparation needed to play one's given roles in life. For now, it is enough to highlight some similarities to the preparation needed to play a role on stage and screen.

Foremost in spiritual preparation is the training of a weak and wandering attention. The first step in such training is learning to concentrate. Then the spiritual aspirant needs to address somatic tension and relaxation of the somatic structure. Learning about attention and relaxation leads organically to self-observation and self-study, which in turn reveals a fragmentation that obtains among the different centers or "brains" in the human structure and the need for their harmonization.

One of the key questions of spiritual life is the matter of feeling, which is approached indirectly through somatic sensation and movement. One discovers that one's usual feeling-states actually impede any reception of the higher influences that can create needed connections among the centers of intelligence.

Finally the question of action and agency, along with allied efforts, needs to be opened and pondered, individually and in group settings, in a school. In order to inhabit a given role consciously the notion of effort, action, and agency must all be questioned and, ultimately, upended decisively. In most schools of inner work movement technologies are employed to assist in opening the question of action and authentic agency.

In addition to this sample of similarities between an acting school and a school of inner work we may find it fruitful to inquire about any correspondence between what an actor seeks and what a spiritual aspirant seeks. In order to explore this question deeply it would also be fruitful to explore what the audience seeks, the "other" in Grotowski's notion of transaction.

Chapter FIVE
THE SEEKING AUDIENCE

An Anomaly

Is tragedy pleasurable? Does the witnessing of extreme situations that produce terrible suffering evoke pleasurable feelings in the audience? Such questions, seemingly outrageous, have been asked seriously by several important thinkers in the history of ideas. For we do see an anomaly: some of the greatest dramas or tragedies, for example *Hamlet* and *King Lear*, bring to the stage horrible suffering and loss, and yet audiences return to view them again and again with satisfaction. How to account for such an anomaly?

Aristotle's View

We have briefly encountered Aristotle's view of tragedy before, so we can reexamine it briefly now. Aristotle accounted for the anomaly by teaching that the audience witnesses extreme situations and suffering with satisfaction because by so witnessing extremity they are purged of negative emotions, specifically the emotions of ruth – wrongly translated as pity – and terror. Insofar as a given individual is so purged, that man or woman is more prepared for a contemplative life which, as the master of a spiritual school called the Lyceum, Aristotle considered to be the only worthwhile life to live. Not all of course who experienced purgation would enter a contemplative way, but at least they would be readied for it. Unlike Plato, Aristotle thought that because of the possibility that certain individuals would incline toward the contemplative life, the presentation of extremity on the stage was worth the risk of glorifying a life of passionate intensity that lacks serenity.

Hume's View

The British empiricist David Hume published a monograph in 1757 called *Four Dissertations,* and one of these "dissertations" or essays is "Of Tragedy." In that essay Hume tries to account for why tragedies are felt to be enjoyable and so repeatable while suffering is experienced as painful and which no sane person would want repeated.

Hume expresses his puzzlement at this enjoyment as an "unaccountable pleasure." He writes that the pleasure is not easy to understand because "sorrow, terror, anxiety, and other passions . . . are in themselves disagreeable and uneasy," a fine example of British understatement.

Hume reviews, and rejects, several attempts to account for the anomaly, one of which is that it transports the audience from a state of indolence and that this is felt to be pleasurable; Hume replies that even if we were bored having to meet a horrid fate would not be pleasurable. We would be cured of the boredom but it would not produce a pleasurable feeling.

Hume's view is that because the audience realizes that the suffering and terror are staged by actors, and so not real, they can be viewed with enjoyment just as viewing a painting of some terrible scene can produce enjoyment. In viewing the tragedy, or the painting, one knows that although the thematic content is terrible the content is not real, and for that reason whatever disagreeable feelings are evoked by such a performance or painting is subsumed within the more dominant feeling of pleasure.

Schopenhauer's View

Hume flourished before Kant; Schopenhauer flourished after Kant, and was in every respect a Kantian. Taking a leaf or two from Kant's third critique, which dealt with art as a reconciling force between the two natures of man, Schopenhauer maintained that art, both in its beautiful and its sublime forms, provided the only comfort and respite available to us from the terror and absurdity of life.

Unlike Kant, Schopenhauer had the great fortune to obtain access to Eastern religious and philosophical thought, although he misread most of that material. His "metaphysical" thought, chastened of course within Kantian limits, posited an unknown and unknowable cosmic Force which he reluctantly called "Will." This Force or life force was indifferent to the plight of men and women, not being any sort of God or personal being. Any trust in or loyalty to this Force was, then, considered inadvisable, according to Schopenhauer. He believed that the Buddha taught a similar doctrine, and that the teaching of the Buddha, along with other Eastern teachers, aligned well with his own attitude toward the world: suffering is caused by desire; to remove suffering desire must be renounced, and in practice Schopenhauer believed this entailed a rejection of the usual will to life, what Nietzsche called a "Buddhistic negation of the will."

Schopenhauer believes that what is presented on stage in a tragedy is so overwhelming that it is much like viewing the sublime in nature: in witnessing a sublime spectacle in nature, for example an overpowering scene, we are reminded of our insignificance and are turned toward a contemplative life, a life such as what the Buddha recommends. Similarly, a tragedy is not beautiful but sublime, and in viewing it, in witnessing the horror and absurdity of existence, we are turned from any love of or attachment to life toward a kind of resignation, toward a life of detachment from this life. Any desire for some sort of poetic justice in dramas or tragedies betrays a lack of understanding about the indifferent Force that informs this world, and yet, despite that indifference, appears to demand our allegiance, our will to live according to its dictates.

In this view Schopenhauer is very close to many Eastern teachings, but his emphasis upon resignation is a Western, not an Eastern, view; it is part of his heritage from Kant, who taught that we must be resigned to not knowing reality, not knowing the truth. Far from teaching resignation, Eastern thought, including the Buddha's, taught various remedies for suffering, which did of course include examining the nature of desire and its role in shaping our identities. Above all, and in contrast to Schopenhauer's rather pessimistic ideas, Eastern thought taught that it is possible to replace ignorance with authentic knowledge.

Nietzsche's View

Nietzsche credited Schopenhauer as being one of his educators while roundly renouncing the latter's ideas about the world. His first book *The Birth of Tragedy* departs from his former teacher in Nietzsche's attempt to account for the anomaly in question.

"How differently Dionysus spoke to me! How far removed from all this resignationism!" Thus spoke Nietzsche when reflecting upon Schopenhauer's view of the anomaly. The tradition of Greek tragedy evolved from festivals devoted to Dionysus, the god of dance, wine, and abandon, of a life affirming vitality that cannot be quenched by the horror and absurdity of life, and it was this spirit, this god, that spoke to Nietzsche.

Nietzsche wrote that the Greeks were profound enough to be deeply moved by life's surds, moved enough to be tempted to what he called a negation of the will to life. The "profound Hellene" was saved from this additional tragedy by art, by the depiction of the horror of life as, despite all appearances to the contrary, "indestructibly powerful and pleasurable." Their art, their tragedies, allowed them to affirm life despite its apparent absurdity and cruelty.

Nietzsche describes Hamlet as the Dionysian man; having obtained knowledge, he is nauseated and unable to find a decent motive for acting, for trying to set an upside down world right side up again. For such a one only art can redeem him from the absurdity of life;

only a Shakespeare can redeem life through the sublimity of his art, presenting the beautiful, creative dimension of life to counter the apparent absurdity and horror. For Nietzsche art is saying yes to life "even in its strangest and hardest problems." When all other action seems not worth taking, the creative act remains as a way to cure one's own world sickness as well as that of others.

Kaufmann's View

Walter Kaufmann, professor of philosophy at Princeton until his untimely death in 1980, published an interesting book on tragedy entitled *Tragedy and Philosophy*; in that work Kaufmann addresses the anomaly we have been exploring, also citing the other thinkers we have considered.

"Suffering shared is suffering halved," is one way Kaufmann puts his argument. When we witness extremity on the stage or screen, we feel that we are not alone; we too suffer, we too face the apparent absurdity of life, and perhaps even with nobility, just as the characters portrayed may do. Our sorrows are presented on stage and in such a way that we feel affirmed not only in our suffering but also in our ability to overcome it with courage.

For Kaufmann tragedy is more hopeful than comedy; in tragedy we do not laugh at virtue and nobility, but in comedy we do. In this regard Greek comedies and the comedies since then up to the 20th century all anticipated the modern and postmodern theatre of the absurd. "Tragedy suggests that nobility is possible . . . . But comedy suggests that nobility is a sham, that courage is preposterous, and that triumphs no less than defeats are ridiculous." Tragedy depends for its effect on empathic feeling for the unfortunate, while comedy depends for its effect on a lack of such feeling, indeed on a streak of cruelty that inhabits us all.

The Author's View

My own view in regard to the anomaly in question rests in part on what we have explored thus far in this book. We have seen how the philosophy of existentialism is the worldview that naturally informs all theatre productions, and that actors and actresses are by nature existential in their chosen professions.

Recall that existentialism is a worldview that begins from extremity, that finds its starting point in the consideration of extreme situations and extreme emotions. Zinn maintains that without the presentation of such extremity the audience will lose interest, turn away from the production as being shallow, not profound, not dealing with the most perplexing questions of life. And that this is because the audience senses on some level that they too are implicated, that they too are involved. This approaches Kaufmann's view, and also helps account for why postmodern approaches like Grotowski's invite more audience participation, treating the audience as the "other" in stage transactions.

Yet I think existentialism has more to say than that. The demand placed upon the actor is the same demand placed upon the audience, and the demand is for a greater participation in life, in ordinary life as well as the life on the stage. In so many ways, several of which we have already considered, the actor must collect himself into a more harmonious state of being in order to portray well an assumed character; similarly, the audience must also collect themselves into a more harmonious state of being in order to benefit from their own participation, in order to feel any sort of "pleasure" or enjoyment.

In ordinary life, for the actor as well as the audience, the three centers of intelligence with which we are most familiar – the intellect, feeling, and sensation-moving – are not connected; they are occupied with their own interests and are not in communication with one another. Despite the fact that actors are counseled to develop an "observer" in themselves, they remain disconnected most of the time. While on stage, however, this disconnection must be, at least for a time, overcome to some degree, much as a musician must harmonize mind, feeling, and body to some extent while performing. The actor seeks for a more unified state of being.

The Audience Seeks

The audience also seeks for this more unified state, a state of intensity and authenticity that almost never obtains in ordinary life: this is why audiences return again and again to view with satisfaction the dramatization of sorrow and horror. They wish to feel more alive, to feel the intensity of what is dramatized. The search of the audience depends upon the search of the actors; the search of the former depends upon the role playing of the latter.

The audience also senses that in some way role playing defines their lives, and that what is presented on stage is somehow a more authentic role playing; somehow more of what is real, more being, is put into the dramatized roles than what is usually possible in ordinary life. Thus the authentic performance of the actor calls to the audience as a challenge and even a demand: to inhabit more authentically the roles that they play. The satisfaction that they feel is the satisfaction of witnessing an authentic playing of a role, sensing that in some sense this authenticity is also possible for them.

The existential actor collects himself into an image of intensity, an image that inspires as emblematic of a fuller life. Few people are willing to place themselves deliberately in extreme situations, though some thrill seekers do. In the theatre more prudent people can experience an intensity seldom met in their lives. This intensity is the heart of the existential worldview. What is missing in it is the equally important experience of serenity.

Chapter SIX

EXISTENTIAL VIRTUE

Virtue In Existential Thought

Philosophies of right vary widely in existential thought, but if one were to choose one English word that captured the spirit of virtue in existentialism it would be authenticity. Authenticity in one form or another is discussed by Kierkegaard, Nietzsche, Jaspers, Heidegger, and Sartre.

For Kierkegaard authenticity means being true to oneself, and that also sums up what being authentic means to the other men cited above. Authenticity carries with it a measure of alienation from others and from the holding culture. And many kinds of fear are also evoked by the notion of being authentic.

Heidegger wrote about the fear of standing out, while Kierkegaard wrote about the fear of making fateful decisions. Nietzsche wrote about the fear of self-critique, and challenged his readers to have the courage, not of one's convictions, but for an attack on one's convictions. Fear of exposure, of standing alone, of making fateful decisions, and of self-inquiry, form the core of those extreme conditions about which existentialists are concerned.

Knowledge

In *The Birth of Tragedy*, Nietzsche disputes any idea that what is needed in facing fear or other extreme conditions is knowledge. He refers to Shakespeare's *Hamlet*, writing that the protagonist, in discovering the truth, by obtaining knowledge, was not able to act decisively, or indeed act at all. Obtaining knowledge just made him nauseated.

For the existentialist, obtaining knowledge about oneself, others, or the world is not liberating, as it appears to be for supposed rationalists like Plato. Nietzsche argues that such faith in rationalism, introduced into the Greek theatre by Euripides, wilted the spirit of music, the Dionysian energy that gave birth to tragedy. Instead what was glorified was the Socratic faith in dialectic.

Socratic dialogue is altogether too tame for the existentialist. What is needed for displaying virtue is a way of life far more intense, far more exciting and adventurous, than the sort of life led in the Greek stoas. What is wanted is the courage to create a life of intensity.

Living Dangerously

Nietzsche maintained that the secret for obtaining the most fulfillment out of life was to live dangerously. "Build your homes on the slopes of Vesuvius!" In saying this Nietzsche was not promoting a foolhardy existence but one that required courage, above all the courage to create.

The ontological need for being, for a fuller immersion in life, is sensed on some level by all of us, and for the existentialist it means to be able to love and create in the face of life's inevitable disappointments and losses. The need for being is what drives audiences to sit through sometimes unbearable scenes of terror, and it is what drives actors and actresses in their wish to inhabit their roles more authentically.

The role of an actor is dangerous, not in a crude sense but in a subtle sense. He invites the position of standing out in a crowd, sometimes literally standing alone, exposing himself to an audience and to his peers. As David Mamet has written, this requires above all courage. Even the most histrionic individual risks exposure on the stage. The actor is continually exposed to critique, and as we have seen he is counseled to critique himself, to develop in himself an "observer" that can monitor his inner and outer life.

All of these elements heighten the actor's sense of alienation, not just from the audience and his peers, but from himself. The latter is perhaps the most dangerous feature of alienation, for self-knowledge produces that feeling of nausea about which existentialists like Sartre write, and does so more effectively and dramatically than any other sort of knowledge.

Art

Nietzsche argued that art saved the Greeks from themselves; through the untamed energy of Dionysus tempered with the imagination of Apollo the "sublime Hellene" was able to project onto the stage the creative intensity needed to reconcile not only the dualism of Dionysus and Apollo but also the fragmented duality of the human being.

The same dynamic obtains for the actor: the only cure for the nausea of self-knowledge is his art; the only cure for his self-alienation is the creative act on the stage. The actor creates himself anew, and of course love is also involved in this creation. Later in the book I will maintain that this creative act is only a temporary salve for nausea and alienation, but for now it suffices to say that for the actor the love poured into his creative act cures, in that moment, the deeply felt nausea produced by the knowledge of the world and of one's self.

Nausea

Sartre temporarily cured his own nausea by writing *Nausea*, one of the 20th century's most profound novels, and also by writing plays like *The Flies* and *No Exit*. But truly there is no permanent exit from the terror and absurdity of life.

No artist has put this absurdity better than Shakespeare's "life is a tale told by an idiot, full of sound and fury, signifying nothing." And part of William Faulkner's novel *The Sound and the Fury*, inspired by Shakespeare's lines, is told by a narrator who is an idiot. Artists in every medium return to their art again and again, seeking relief from nausea, just as actors return again and again to newer roles and audiences return repeatedly to the theatre.

Kierkegaard wrote about "the sickness unto death," or despair, and Sartre wrote that life begins on the other side of despair. Existentialists begin with despair, but they end with courage, creativity, and love. Although there is no real cure for the nausea of despair, there is relief in the creation and contemplation of art.

The Contemplation Of Art

Although not considered an existentialist, Schopenhauer dealt with a number of existentialist themes. He maintained that the only respite we have from the absurdity of life is the contemplation of art. We have already seen how Schopenhauer argued that audiences enjoy plays that depict such absurdity, whether tragedy, comedy, or a combination of the two, because they are able to withdraw their interest from such absurdity, becoming more detached from life and its surds.

I have already written that this view cannot fully account for why audiences enjoy the portrayal of sometimes terrible, often absurd, events. In effect audiences sense what the actor is doing on stage: creating for himself a more unified state of being, one that gathers his usually scattered attention into a more powerful, authentic expression. Far from wishing to withdraw their being-energy from life, the audience wishes to emulate the actor by experiencing a more unified state themselves. Of course they are not aware of this wish on a conscious level; as soon as they rise from their theatre seats they once more enter the common state of fragmentation and ignorance of their habitual state of being.

The Actor's Creation

The actor is also unaware of what he is actually creating, so lost is he in more surface manifestations. To be sure, the actor is seeking relief from nausea, but on an even deeper level he is seeking a fuller life, a more profound immersion in being.

The actor's creation, on the surface, is the creation of a character, an interpretation of what the playwright has written for that particular part in the play. The deeper creation, the redemptive act, is the creation of a more unified state of being, a more profound immersion in life itself. All of an actor's training, all his preparation, both in acting school and in assuming a particular part or character, is leading to this most important creative act.

It is this creation that so captivates his peers and the audience. His peers on stage do care about the more surface creation, insofar as it affects their own performance, but the audience has no investment in that creation; what moves the audience, and ultimately his peers, is the creation of a new and compelling state of being, a more harmonious functioning that matches the extremity of the drama itself, the manifestation of a far more profound immersion in being than almost any other example one could adduce in ordinary life. The virtue of the existentialist actor is an immersion in intensity.

Intensity

The playwright, director, and performers know that a given play, to be successful, must call all participants, on and off stage, to an intense state of being. The stakes before the characters in the play must be high, matters of life and death. In melodramatic movies, saving the world is a common theme. In more quality productions it is not the world that is in danger of falling but rather the vital lie that is human character.

The quality play is indeed an imitation of life, for it mimics the actual ontological dilemma of the human being: in order to save himself, the human being must have more being. In order to save himself from perishing in the vital lie of character or personality, the human being must collect himself into a more authentic state of being human. Only then is he able to receive salvific help from the cosmos. For in this more collected state he begins to be noticed as a recognizable force, an actual force of nature, standing in between cosmic energies and able to assimilate and transmit the life-force, the force of Being itself.

Thus the actor is an unwitting imitator of the ontological or spiritual aspirant: in order to save himself, in order to save both the character and his portrayal of same, the actor must collect himself into a more authentic state of being human. And the audience is an unwitting participant in this drama because the individuals comprising it know that they too must be saved, must collect themselves into a more authentic state.

So it is that in referring to the existentialist virtue one may use the word intense as a synonym for the word authentic. To be authentic is to be collected into a more harmonious state, and to be collected is to be intense. Such intensity is the Dionysian being to which Nietzsche refers as the womb from which tragedy as an art form was born. Dionysus refers to that force of nature which can well up from below and manifest in drunken, frenzied states of being, yet it also refers to that same force that can descend from above, if and only if a more harmonious connection is made among the centers of intelligence in a given human being. This connection is needed for authentic creativity.

Creation

The creations of artists are imitations of authentic creativity, exemplified above all in the witting, or unwitting, creation of an authentic human being. This imitation is unwitting, and is usually taken to be authentic creativity. The only genuine creation is creation from above, given if and only if one is connected inside.

The same consideration applies to the actor's art: the actor unwittingly imitates the authentic creation that is taking place even as he engages the more superficial creation of a role. But authentic creation without knowledge is dependent upon the exigencies of circumstance. In this regard the needed element in real creativity is knowledge.

Full Circle

With the question of knowledge we have come full circle from where we started exploring the existential virtue. For the existentialist, epitomized by Nietzsche, knowledge results in nausea, in alienation, and indeed this result is what we find in ancient tragedy. Oedipus persists in obtaining knowledge and in so doing brings disaster upon himself and his community. In Elizabethan tragedy too we find Hamlet and Lear both coming to grief upon obtaining knowledge.

But this sort of knowledge is not authentic knowledge, as Socrates and Plato knew. Although such "knowledge" can have a devastating impact upon individuals and communities, it is a relatively unimportant sort of information that need not bring one to grief. As Socrates taught, authentic knowledge yields happiness, a freedom from knowledge so called. Knowledge or understanding of the authentic kind frees one from the nausea produced by the inauthentic kind. The fears that plague those who react to inauthentic knowledge evaporate before the understanding produced by authentic knowledge.

Authentically Human

Authentic knowledge creates the authentic human being. Existential thought, in failing to understand knowledge, is reduced to accepting an ersatz nobility, an inauthentic humanity that betrays human potential. In so doing existential thought fails to live up to its proclaimed virtue: authenticity. What remains is intensity without authenticity, an intensity which, although inspiring, misleads those who fall under its spell. In claiming to be authentic, such intensity is as beguiling as it is bewitching.

Hence the existential actor, though collecting himself into a more unified state of being, is still inauthentic insofar as he is dependent upon his art for salvation. This "salvation," far from being completely transformative, is incomplete even in its creative moments. For authentic creativity and humanity understanding is needed, an understanding produced by a knowledge without quotation marks.

Chapter SEVEN
THE SPIRITUAL SCHOOL

The Search For Knowledge

The search for knowledge in a school of inner work runs counter to all other forms of knowledge acquisition; knowledge in such a school is not understood as knowledge obtained in a scholarly or scientific sense. Instead, knowledge is understood as being, and an increase of knowledge on any level is an increase in being.

This understanding is of course not understood in the holding culture; that is why a school is needed, because those just entering the school have been conditioned to believe that knowledge is a subject knowing some object of information, and that what distinguishes knowledge from belief is that the former requires some kind of warrant or justification to be accepted as true. In a school of spiritual or ontological development to know is to be, without remainder.

What Is Truth?

The question that Pilate is supposed to have asked Jesus is hardly original with him; philosophers and other thinkers have been asking that question for millennia. The answer that spiritual schools through the ages have given is not so much what truth is as what it is not: truth is not propositional; it is not something that can be captured conceptually.

Plato, the founder of one of the earliest schools, the Academy, wrote several dialogues in which his teacher, Socrates, challenged those who thought they knew the answer to that question, and who thought it could be stated with words. Western philosophy, in particular Nietzsche and his epigones, believes that Socrates was a rationalist, one who thinks that truth can be known by the ordinary mind and expressed adequately in language. This belief is a fundamental error in judgment, an inability to distinguish between knowledge so called and authentic knowledge.

A spiritual school is intended to wean participants from ersatz knowledge to an understanding of real knowledge. Socrates said that "I know [real knowledge] that I know [ersatz knowing] nothing." Ersatz knowledge is simply ignorance: ignorance about how the mind actually works to obtain authentic knowledge or understanding.

How The Mind Works

Western philosophy and psychology misunderstand the most fundamental operation of the mind. This most fundamental function is an unconscious process of desire, a process of identification. It is a process that begins with the naming of a child; from there the child identifies with the name and all that follows in its train.

Philosopher Saul Kripke has revolutionized much of ordinary language philosophy with his notion of naming and necessity; he argues that there is no conceptual web between us and reality, as other philosophers have maintained, but that through naming, for example a child, we have direct contact with the real. Nixon would still be Nixon in any possible world, whereas the statement "Nixon was implicated in Watergate" might not be the case in another possible world. Therefore Nixon is a necessary truth in all possible worlds.

If naming indeed provides necessary truth and directly contacts the real it is an odd truth and an ersatz real. It is just such an idea of reality that spiritual schools wish to upend. The naming of a child is only the beginning of the conceptual morass in which we are immersed. The fact that I have a name leads me to believe in my socially constructed self, just that self that a school of inner work leads me to question and eventually discard. Our logic and language complete the seduction, and it takes an organized school even to begin to challenge these falsehoods. Nixon is indeed a true name in all possible worlds, but the name "Nixon" and indeed all names and concepts, far from contacting the real, contact only seductive substitutes for reality. The negative judgment of Kant regarding knowing the real remains.

An Aspirant Prepares

How, then, can a spiritual aspirant in a school of inner work know the real? Through an extended process of preparation, lasting many years. Just as an actor must prepare to play different roles on stage, so must a spiritual seeker prepare to receive the knowledge or being needed to grow ontologically.

The first step is to learn to appreciate the value of attention. For it is through attention that all subsequent knowledge will be obtained. The next step is to begin to learn about one's actual condition, including the fact of fragmentation and the concomitant fact of a false belief in one's unity and continuity. Like the preparation of an actor, a spiritual aspirant must learn to collect himself using his attention, must concentrate his attention and in so doing bring his head, heart, and body into closer alignment, eventually into connection with one another.

Again like an actor, exercises are given to further this education: physical exercises, movements, exercises to train the attention and during which one can begin to verify the ideas given in a school that challenge all the mistaken notions of the holding culture. One begins to learn that there is not a unity of being that is suggested by one's name, but that what obtains in truth is a collection of roles or "subpersonalities" that claim the status of 'I' or a real self only so long as one of them is needed; when that role is temporarily ended another rises to take its place, depending upon the conditions that are presented and that must be negotiated.

The Role Of Roles

The role of roles is pretty much as Freud described the purpose of the psychoanalytical ego: to negotiate consensus reality. Even on an ordinary level, and without the benefit of a school, we sense that we need to adopt different roles in varied settings. Roles are adopted or learned in differing communities of people, the first of course being one's family of origin. In a spiritual school, the most instructive role to be studied, the one that begins to open the door to authentic self-inquiry, is the role adopted in the school itself.

Depending upon one's age in entering a school of inner work, one brings with one a collection of learned roles, conditioned above all by the earliest roles learned as a child. During the process of forming an ego or "self" in a socially conditioned sense one is subjected to the formation of a foundational core, around which one's other parts revolve as a wheel about an axle. These other parts, subpersonalities, or roles are decisively conditioned by this foundational part, and in engaging in the self-inquiry characteristic of a spiritual school one is led inexorably to its discovery and continued exposure.

Clues to this center of one's acquired nature begin to accumulate as one begins the process of adopting roles in the school. More ambitious individuals, for example, may eagerly take on roles that require considerable responsibility in the functioning of the school; more reticent individuals will likely wish to remain unnoticed, participating actively while avoiding any limelight. Rebellious individuals may set up perplexing roadblocks to their own development. And so on. Continuing to cite examples would be pointless, the main point being that one's self-study, one's self-inquiry, is best conducted by studying the roles adopted in the school.

Self-Inquiry

Although the discovery of one's acquired center is important, it constitutes only a small part of self-inquiry in a school of inner discovery and development. The lion's share of such inquiry is in questioning one's usual sense and feeling of identity.

The exploration of one's assumed roles in a school of inner work leads organically into a study of one's assumed roles in life outside the school. The usual view of oneself as a single individual or entity putting on and taking off roles as an actor does costumes begins to weaken as it becomes more and more apparent that life roles constitute a discrete set of "subpersonalities" or identities that in no way add up to a single, continuous, individual entity or self. What begins slowly to emerge into awareness is a collection of discrete *activities* that we call roles, and that what obtains in our acquired nature is not a real self or entity but a useful set of activities that in a deeper sense are a bit too useful: they have deceived us into believing we already possess a unified being, a self, and that we are authentic agents.

Fragmentation

We have seen how human beings all sense that what is needed is a more unified state of being, a more harmonious way of living that is considered more authentic or intense. In the world of acting, of theatre, this need for greater being drives actors and audiences alike. In a spiritual school serious self-inquiry invariably leads to the at first dispiriting discovery of inner fragmentation.

Here we have an example of how authentic knowledge is required to satisfy the wish for greater, more unified being. Knowledge of fragmentation, initially experienced as an unwelcome revelation, is ultimately seen as salvific when combined with the knowledge of what awaits the aspirant once fragmentation is overcome. For what is also revealed is how a harmonious connection among usually disconnected parts can invite the creative process needed to develop into a state of authentic humanity, combining intensity and serenity.

Intensity

We have seen that audiences are captivated by the presentation of intensity on the stage or on screen, and that actors and actresses likewise inspired strive to portray such intensity. What is not understood by actor and audience alike is that intensity is only one half of an authentic state of being.

Actually the tragic form of drama and literature should have been instructive all along, but very few have noticed that. Aristotle, being one of the very few, characterized tragic "heroes" as being only of "middling" virtue, and by that he was not saying such characters were not admirable; rather, he was saying that to be virtuous one must reconcile intensity with serenity.

Tragic heroes come to grief precisely because of their intensity, and playwrights like Aeschylus call attention to the need for less willfulness and more justice. Likewise Plato calls for the development of justice in *The Republic*, not just in civil society but above all in the individual human being. And for the development of justice an equal measure of intensity and serenity is indispensable.

Serenity

Intensity calls for a fuller immersion in life, and demands a collected attention that allows a coming together of the different centers of intelligence: mind, body, and feeling. Yet intensity alone, without knowledge, cannot last, and cannot be lastingly transformative.

Knowledge obtained in a spiritual school enables one to see the futility of intensity without knowledge. For intensity without knowledge is like the extremity of Dionysus, full of life but undirected and so misdirected. Extremity may be courted in all sorts of crude and dangerous ways, including risking one's life and risking the lives of others. Even exceptional human beings like Oedipus and Hamlet can be led astray by the intensity of their passions. Most tragic of all, intensity without authentic knowledge is prey to inauthentic knowledge, the ultimately destructive "knowledge" that leads to nausea and a life hell bent on overcoming nausea.

If one enters a school of inner work with such an upset stomach, the knowledge obtained there will quickly relieve it. The existentialist view of the absurdity of existence is replaced with the saner view of existence as a school of self-development, leading one to the goal of liberation from misguided ways of being in the world. The school is a transformative community of seekers, supporting one another in gradually incorporating an altogether new understanding.

The heart of this new way of being is the force of attention, able to reconcile intensity and serenity. Schools of acting also recognize the importance of attention, but their teachings do not explicitly instruct actors about the need *simultaneously* to be aware of themselves and whatever might be their focus of attention outside themselves. The focus of attention outside oneself is usually the attention needed to concentrate on the action at hand on stage, and this requirement, plus the usually unwitting inner collectivity, is enough for acting purposes. But for the purpose of inner growth of being, the act of inner collection must precede the outer action; indeed, this former act is the only real activity.

Serenity is the result of an action initiated from above the usual sense and feeling of oneself. The force of attention is one's ownmost force or energy, having many levels and qualities. This force is able to allow a connection to be formed between the mind and the body; this connection calls the feeling and, with that connection, a door is opened to a higher awareness, an energy that provides the only authentic creative agency and which in its turn begins the slow but sure process of the discovery and development of being.

Intensity immerses one in life; serenity oversees this immersion. One cannot reconcile intensity and serenity conceptually; the attempt to do so only issues in paradox. The apparent paradox is dissolved in immediate experience. What Descartes called "presence to consciousness" is all that is needed.

Extremity

The existential approach to intensity, in ordinary life and in the profession of acting, requires extremity; the existential actor, in life and on stage, begins in the midst of extreme conditions, situations, or emotions. At stake is the vital lie that is character; to preserve that lie the actor must pass through the fires of extremity. If he survives the ordeal without either crossing over into madness or death, he may be said to be living on the other side of extremity, as Sartre put it in speaking of despair. But the alternative to this ordeal is a living death.

The usual approach to life squanders a precious opportunity. The Buddhists speak about the "precious human body," the golden opportunity presented in a human incarnation. A life without intensity, without passion, is a living death, and those who attend theatrical performances sense that, sense that their own lives are frittered away in tepid amusements and ignoble aspirations. They desire intensity but also fear it, and with good reason. For intensity poses a danger to the vital lie of character; it threatens to shatter it in a flood of extremity, and even if it remains intact it fears another ordeal, from which it may not recover.

The precious opportunity is to discover another alternative, an intensity, a nobility, that not only shatters the vital lie of character but that also preserves and develops what is real in us, the real being. The discovery is that the lie is only a shell designed to protect the real, and with the shattering of the shell it is seen that the shell is not needed, that indeed it is the chief obstacle to the discovery of authenticity. It is the dragon guarding the hoard of gold, the beast that must be slain.

The risk is there either way: either one risks shattering the lie with intensity alone, or one risks shattering the lie with intensity and serenity. The former wastes our precious human bodies; the latter turns them into transformative athanors.

Chapter EIGHT
AUTHENTIC AGENCY

Acting

What is authentic acting, authentic agency? The profession of acting provides numerous clues, aside from what science may teach us about agency. But first we do need to consider scientific accounts of agency, and perhaps philosophical accounts as well.

Science generally teaches that every event has a cause, at least on the macro level of physical reality. The science of psychology, which best describes human behavior, agrees. Here events are called actions, and causes are called motivations. Philosophy since Kant has resigned itself to a respectful agnosticism regarding human agency; Hume called into doubt the very concept of causation, and Kant saved it as a scientific concept by saying that it is a necessary category of the mind, just as space and time are. Science, then, is chastened by critical or Kantian philosophy as a description of how things must appear to us, not as an explanation of how things really are.

So too the science of psychology: it describes the way things appear to be in accounting for human agency. And things appear to be the following, for psychology: human agency is caused by motivations. In order to describe events scientifically, actions must be determined by causes or motivations. Free will as commonly accepted is an illusion; no act can occur without a motive, a cause. Free choice is an illusion; if I choose one thing over another it is because I have a motive for doing so. My choice is determined by my motive or motives. If I have difficulty making a choice it is because I have conflicting motives, but the strongest motive or desire will always win. There is simply no room for freedom in a scientific accounting of human agency.

This strict determinism is clearest in the behaviorist school of psychology. Behaviorism is the best example of a psychology that accounts for "man the machine," but other schools of psychology do as well. Psychodynamic psychology, initiated by Freud, is just as deterministic in its theoretical formulations. The existentialist school of psychology may follow Sartre in proclaiming that men and women are "condemned to be free," but the sort of "freedom" that existentialists speak and write about is not any sort of freedom from determining conditions. On the contrary, it is a "freedom" compatible with determinism, and is indeed the only sort of freedom that makes sense on the level of human agency.

This "compatibilist" version of freedom is presented in the following way. To have any sort of freedom as an agent is not freedom from determining conditions; it is not freedom from motivations, which would be an incoherent view of freedom. Rather, it is freedom from coercion. When Sartre says that we are condemned to be free, he means that we are condemned to make fateful decisions, and this "freedom" causes dread, fear of an extreme nature. We must make decisions for ourselves, and this decision making may have fateful consequences for ourselves and others. But each decision we make is determined by motivations; each decision is determined by causes, just as every other event is. People who believe that making decisions is proof of freedom from causation have not thought the notion of agency through but have accepted a pervasive cultural myth as truth. The freedom of which existentialists speak and write is completely compatible with scientific determinism.

Thus to be free is not to be coerced. Prisoners have lost a measure of their freedom because they are forced to remain in prison. People who feel oppressed usually believe that they are coerced in some way that deprives them of their freedom to act as they would prefer acting. If I hand over my money to a mugger I cannot be charged with acting freely; I rightly feel forced to act in a way I would not otherwise act. My actions are not determined by my own wishes or preferences but by the coercive actions taken by the mugger. It could of course still be argued that I am free to refuse to hand over my money, but a court of law, or a court of sensible opinion, would agree that as a practical matter I am not free; I am being coerced. Perhaps a better example would be the contrast between jumping through a window and being thrown through a window: in the former case I am acting on my motivations; in the latter I am not. The latter case is clearly not a free act on my part.

Acting On Stage

Let us return to the acting profession for some aforementioned clues as to the nature of authentic agency. Requirements for authentic acting on stage include concentrated attention, relaxation of tension, self-inquiry or self-study, and above all well considered actions that evoke the appropriate emotional state.

Although these methods of preparation are necessary, what produces compelling acting on stage is the gathering together of the human energies that are usually dispersed. Authentic acting on stage is the result of a collected state of intensity that unwittingly mimics what authentic acting would be in ordinary life. While remembering his conventional identity, the actor gathers all his energetic parts for the sake of an authentic performance, a performance during which he consciously plays a role.

Such consciousness or awareness is key. The role is given: the playwright has written the lines and the actor must say them, along with the actions and emotions that cohere with them. All the actor has to bring to the role is himself, and more than his actions, more than his emotions, more than the lines delivered, is his awareness. Every character created by playwrights has motivations that determine what they say and do, that determine their actions. This fact of psychology does not constitute authentic agency. Authentic agency, authentic freedom, is an act *anterior* to the actions observed on stage. Authentic agency is an *awareness* of motivated actions, both within the actor and without as staged actions.

Consciously Playing A Role

Consciously playing a role constitutes authentic agency and freedom, both on stage and in ordinary life. Without the knowledge needed to discriminate between one's authentic identity and the roles played in life, it is not possible to play a role consciously. In the case of an actor, the challenge is to discriminate between his conventional identity and the role he is playing on stage; in the case of an aspirant in a spiritual school, the challenge is to remember her real Identity as she plays her varied roles consciously.

In our daily lives we may dimly perceive that we are playing varied roles depending upon the situation or environs, but our equally dim recognition of who we "really" are constitutes not knowledge but ignorance. Because of this ignorance it is all too easy to lose ourselves in our roles, particularly if we have invested our sense of who we are in them. It would be like an actor who loses himself in a staged role; his performance would suffer and his peers and the audience would detect this loss as an inauthentic portrayal. They would no longer be inspired by an authentic agency but would instead witness the more usual state of unwitting, mechanical action.

Authentic Freedom

The only sensible sort of freedom describable by science and philosophy is compatible with determinism. Yet in the history of philosophy thinkers have posited a kind of freedom from motivations. Insofar as this freedom is supposed to occur on the level of action, it is false; there is no place for it on that level. Kant posited a freedom to will the good, and he maintained that this freedom was on another plane or level entirely, one that transcended the level of action or so called agency.

Kant transmitted into philosophy the ancient teaching of the two natures of man: a lower nature, comprising our conditioning and all other acquired features, and a higher nature, our connection with the *noumenon*, that unknown Force or Energy in which our higher nature participates and by which our higher nature acts. Schopenhauer called this Force "Will"; he did so reluctantly because he did not want to confuse a word like "Force" or "Energy" with scientific concepts of force or energy. But he did mean something more like an unknown Force than an unknown Will. Action proceeding from this unknown Source, according to Kant, is the only authentic agency.

Thus true freedom, real agency, and authentic will come from and are sourced in the unknown and unknowable Reality, according to Kant and Schopenhauer. When Kant wrote that phenomena are caused by the unknown, the "things in themselves," Schopenhauer chided him for sneaking the notion of causation in the back door; Kant taught that causation applied to the world of appearance only, the world of phenomena, and yet here he was saying that the unknown caused the known. Schopenhauer wrote that this was the wrong way to try to describe authentic agency. The Unknown is beyond cause, as it is beyond space and time and the other categories of human understanding.

Kant wanted somehow to point in words to the Unknown, but could not improve upon Descartes' "presence to consciousness." The Unknown, the Force creating and sustaining the cosmos, is the one constant in human experience, the only constant: Being itself, Awareness itself, Consciousness itself. All phenomena arise and fall, manifest and pass away, but Awareness, Being, does not arise, nor does it pass away; it is always already the case. Though always present, it is an unknown Force; though always constant, it is unknown and by and large unnoticed.

Authentic agency is an act by the unknown Agent, constantly aware, seldom recognized. The nature of this Agent is to pour itself into created or emergent forms in an act of involution; when this act reaches its nadir, the act of evolution begins, an act of returning to Itself. In the human form the Agent wills a part of that form, a part of

Itself, to forget Itself and then remember Itself; this process of hide and seek is part of what is required to maintain and rejuvenate the created or emergent order. Blended energies of different levels keep the cosmos going and growing.

The Human Form

In the human form this act is too obvious to be noticed readily or easily. The Agent is willing to awaken to itself in a given human form and calls to the human being to begin the process of stirring from sleep. Obstacles to awakening and to obtaining authentic knowledge include somatic tensions, egoistic feelings, and thoughts, but above all the ordinary sense and feeling of identity, the socially conditioned and acquired feeling of self.

The act of acting provides important clues to the overcoming of these obstacles. Both actor and audience intuit that their usual sense and feeling of self are incomplete and somehow lacking in sufficient life, sufficient intensity. In order to generate this sufficiency, the actor must awaken to some degree this usually latent force within himself called attention. He must gather his energies, muster his inner resources, and present on stage something more like an authentic human being. Likewise the audience, though to a lesser degree, must gather themselves into enough of a real individual to be able to correspond in however marginal a way to the action on stage.

Yet it is not the outer action on stage that is decisive or creative in this process; it is the inner act, prior to all outer actions, that comprises the real creative action. Not the actual playing of the role, but the act of collecting oneself into a more coherent human being is the action that is most compelling to the audience because it is that act that provides the most dramatic and intense outer actions. The Agent in the actor calls to the Agent in the audience.

Agency In Role Playing

Plato feared the glorification of a life of intensity without serenity that the stage usually dramatizes. Although there is much to be cautious about on this score, Aristotle was also right in believing that the drama could be an awakening influence. For stage acting is emblematic of what is not only possible but also desirable in ordinary life: a more intense life, not due to passion but due to a more unified state of being.

Aristotle missed the mark in emphasizing that the audience, in being purged of unwanted emotion, would incline to the contemplative life. The spiritual influence of the stage is rather the presentation of what a more gathered attention might yield: an opening to the authentic Agent and so the embodiment of authentic agency.

The playing of roles in ordinary life is something all reasonably intelligent and sensitive people do as a matter of course. The *conscious* playing of roles, informed by knowledge, however, is seldom undertaken. And that is because it takes a thorough reeducation and retraining in a spiritual school to obtain the needed knowledge.

Knowledge begins with the slowly dawning understanding that one's usual identity is not an entity but an activity: the activity of avoiding the real, avoiding what is. Some spiritual traditions teach there is no lower self, some teach that there are many selves, 'I's, or subpersonalities rather than a single, unified 'I.' These so called little 'I's are really just a collection of roles, and rather than reifying them by referring to them as bogus identities it is better to represent them to ourselves as differing roles. By so doing we can view them as different *activities* rather than different entities.

There is only one Self, the Agent of change, of transformation. And there is only one act, the serene act of oversight, of awareness. This authentic act effects immediate change in the human form by allowing the usually disconnected energies of the human structure to come together, in turn inviting the creative process within the human athanor. The only creative act is the awareness of role playing.

Awareness Of Role Playing

In ordinary life one could argue that one hardly needs a school of inner work to be aware that one is playing a role on one occasion and a different role on another. There is some truth to that argument, so, to clarify, I need to explain the difference between ordinary awareness and the awareness needed to be aware of the significance of role playing.

The major difference is knowledge. Without knowledge, one cannot be expected to understand the significance of role playing itself, nor of the need for an awareness of it. The ordinary individual misunderstands the significance of role playing; such a person believes that one's presentation must alter depending upon the circumstances, and that one cannot play the same role at work, say, that one plays at a social gathering or at church. For such an individual the significance of role playing amounts to a practical adjustment of one's presentation to the world; it does not in any way affect one's conventional identity, which by and large remains the same in the mind of that man or woman.

In a spiritual school, one learns that this conventional identity is itself comprised of all the roles one plays in life. One also learns that these roles have a deeper purpose than simply presenting a proper façade to the world; they are primarily created for the purpose of avoiding reality. And the most immediate reality being avoided is that there is no self or entity using all these roles for its own purposes; instead, the supposed self is just and only this collection of roles, all combining in an artificial way to create the illusion of unity and continuity. One role wheels in and another wheels out, in its turn to be replaced by a third role. And so on. The illusion is that there is a self, an ontological entity, behind all these roles and directing the show. The reality is that the roles wheel in and out with such rapidity that an illusion of selfhood is created, much like the whirling of a lit sparkler creates the illusion of a fiery circle.

When the spiritual aspirant learns and becomes convinced that the putative self is a collection of activities rather than an entity, she begins to realize that with no ontological entity there is quite literally no one to do anything. And that all the activity is designed, unwittingly, to avoid discovering this rather unsettling truth. The clothes have no emperor. And with no one to do anything, one becomes more interested in what possibility there is first, to have an identity and, then, actually to do, actually to act. In order to act, there must be an agent. One wonders: is agency, then, at all possible?

Such questioning leads inexorably to enough discovery and development to supply the needed knowledge. The real Identity reveals itself, and with that revelation comes the realization that this Self is the Agent, the Source of authentic agency and so the Initiator of the only free act: an awareness of what is, an awareness of Awareness, or, simply, Awareness itself. Knowledge and Being are one and the same act: to know is to be; to be is to know. And Being is the energetic mate of the stillness of Awareness; in mythological terms, the marriage of Shiva and Shakti, stillness and energy.

Awareness, then, oversees role playing, understanding it as the conditioning with which men and women negotiate consensus reality. The ersatz self has been found out, revealed as a collection of useful roles. And finally, after many years, Awareness reveals itself as all and everything, the one Energy taking all forms.

Awareness, the Self, is the Cosmic Actor, playing all roles, calling its audience to join in the cosmic dance, to participate actively in the cosmic theatre.

The Immortality Project

The inauthentic immortality project is the futile attempt by human beings to deny their mortality. Existentialists like Becker have long ago diagnosed this malady without, however, proposing a viable cure. The cure for this project is confined to esoteric, spiritual schools.

The attempt to deny mortality is just another example of the futile attempt to avoid reality. The fact that the human form will die is as inescapable as any other fact of reality. The countless activities of what we may with permission call the ego or conditioned sense of self are all efforts to escape the inescapable. In order to approach the authentic immortality project all such activity must cease. One must come to a profound inner stillness.

An authentic immortality project involves the only truly creative act: the creation, by the Agent of change, of a new, second body that will survive the death of the first, physical body. This creation is the fulfillment of human life at this level of the created or emergent order. It is a development or evolution of being well beyond that envisaged by modern developmental psychology. Tibetan Buddhists speak of the rainbow body, Sufis speak of the body of light, Taoists speak of the *ling* or "soul," Christian esoterics speak of the resurrection body, elders in the school of Gurdjieff speak of the energetic body or the body of sensation. In every authentic spiritual tradition some mention is made of an energetic human form created within the physical body, oven, or athanor, accomplished by first stilling egoic activity and then allowing authentic agency to work the miracle of transformation.

The hard truth is that we are nothing and can do nothing. But this applies only to our illusions of self and agency. The higher truth is that we have the potential to correspond to the structure of the cosmos in every respect, including Self and agency, and that we are invited to fulfill our destiny to become immortal in our ongoing service to the whole.

We are invited to die before we die, to die to the illusion of selfhood and agency. The so called death of the ego is not the death of any entity; it is the effective stilling of the futile activity of avoiding reality. It is not the end of role playing but the end of unconscious role playing. With the death of the illusion of self comes the recognition of the reality of Self, and with that the realization that the Self is always already playing all possible roles. In adopting conscious role playing we align ourselves with the authentic activity of the Self and so become in truth Microcosmic Man.

BIBLIOGRAPHY

Abel, Lionel. *Metatheatre*. Hill & Wang, NY, 1963.

Adler, Stella. *On the Technique of Acting*. Bantam, NY, 1988.

Aeschylus. *The Oresteian Trilogy*. Penguin, Harmondsworth, 1956.

Aristotle. *Poetics*. Dover, NY, 1951.

Auerbach, Erich. *Mimesis*. Anchor, NY, 1957.

Becker, Ernest. *The Denial of Death*. Free Press, NY, 1973.

Blumenfeld, Robert. *Stagecraft*. Limelight, Milwaukee, 2011.

Bowra, Maurice. *Sophoclean Tragedy*. Clarendon, Oxford, 1965.

Brecht, Bertolt. *Brecht on Theatre*. Hill & Wang, NY, 1964.

Brook, Peter. *Leaning on the Moment*. Parabola, NY, 1979.

_____. *The Empty Space*. Touchstone, NY, 1968.

Bryant, Gary. *Invicti Solis*. Balboa, Bloomington, 2015.

_____. *The Liberation of Thought*. Balboa, Bloomington, 2015.

_____. *The Sickness of Effort*. Balboa, Bloomington, 2016.

Camus, Albert. *The Fall*. Knopf, NY, 1957.

Chekhov, Michael. *The Path of the Actor*. Routledge, NY, 2005.

Cooper, Lane. *The Poetics of Aristotle*. Cooper, NY, 1963.

Dennet, Daniel. *Elbow Room*. Bradford, Cambridge, 2015.

De Salzmann, Jeanne. *The Reality of Being*. Shambhala, Boston, 2010.

Dodds, E.R. *The Greeks and the Irrational*. Beacon, Boston, 1957.

Else, Gerald. *The Origin and Early Form of Greek Tragedy*.
Harvard, Cambridge, 1965.

Esper, William & DiMarco, Darmon. *The Actor's Art and Craft*. Anchor,
NY, 2008.

Euripides. *Ten Plays*. Bantam, NY, 1960.

Fergusson, Francis. *The Idea of a Theatre*. Anchor, NY, 1953.

Grotowski, Jerzy. *Towards a Poor Theatre*. Preface by Peter Brook.
Routledge, NY, 2002.

Hadot, Pierre. *What Is Ancient Philosophy?* Belknap, Cambridge, 2002.

Harris, Sam. *Free Will*. Free Press, NY, 2012.

Homer. *The Iliad*. Penguin, Harmondsworth, 1950.

Hume, David. *Four Dissertations*. Millar, London, 1757.

Jones, Earnest. *Hamlet and Oedipus*. Norton, NY, 1949.

Kaufmann, Walter. *Existentialism from Dostoevsky to Sartre*. Meridian,
NY, 1956.

_____. *Tragedy and Philosophy*. Princeton, 1979.

Kierkegaard, Soren. *The Concept of Dread*. Princeton, 1968.

Kitto, H.D.F. *Greek Tragedy*. Anchor, NY, 1950.

Laing, R.D. *The Divided Self*. Penguin, Baltimore, 1965.

Lecog, Jacques. *The Moving Body*. Routledge, NY, 2000.

Linklater, Kristin. *Freeing the Natural Voice*. TCG, NY, 1992.

Murray, Gilbert. *Aeschylus*. Clarendon, Oxford, 1962.

Nietzsche, Friedrich. *The Birth of Tragedy*. Random, NY, 1968.

Ouspensky, P.D. *In Search of the Miraculous*. Harvest, NY, 1977.

Plato. *The Dialogues*. Random, NY, 1937.

Rowan, John. *Subpersonalities*. Routledge, NY, 1990.

Sartre, Jean Paul. *Nausea*. New Directions, Norfolk, 1949.

_____. *Existentialism and Humanism*. Nagel, Paris, 1946.

_____. *No Exit and Three Other Plays*. Vintage, NY, 1958.

Schopenhauer, Arthur. *The World as Will and Representation*. Falcon's Wing, Indian Hills, 1958.

Shaw, George Bernard. *The Quintessence of Ibsenism*. Toronto, 1979.

_____. *Man and Superman*. Dodd, NY, 1928.

Sophocles. *The Oedipus Cycle*. Harvest, NY, n.d.

Stanislavski, Constantin. *An Actor Prepares*. Routledge, NY, 1989.

Steiner, George. *The Death of Tragedy*. Knopf, NY, 1961.

Whitman, Cedric. *Sophocles*. Harvard, Cambridge, 1951.

Whitman, Robert. *Shaw and the Play of Ideas*. Cornell, Ithaca, 1977.

ABOUT THE AUTHOR

Gary Bryant is an ordained priest, a hospice chaplain, and a lifetime student of dramatic theory and practice. He has several graduate degrees, having studied at Rice University, The University of Chicago, and Harvard University. Gary is also the author of a trilogy published by Balboa Press, *Invicti Solis*, *The Liberation of Thought*, and *The Sickness of Effort*. *Role Playing* is intended to be a continuation of that trilogy, all four books designed to explore the universal search for liberation and immortality.

With 30 years experience in spiritual traditions, Gary is also interested in how best to connect the world of being and the world of daily living.

He is also past President of The Prometheus Society, past Membership Officer of The Triple Nine Society, former associate of the International Society for Philosophical Enquiry (ISPE), former lifetime member of Mensa, and a current member of the on line Four Sigma Society.

Gary enjoys participating in athletic activities with his wife, with whom he resides in the Houston metro area.

Printed in the United States
By Bookmasters